IMPRESSIONISM

A clear insight into Artists and their Art

Pam Cutler

Barrington Stoke

First published 2004 in Great Britain by
Barrington Stoke Ltd, Sandeman House, Trunk's Close,
55 High Street, Edinburgh, EH1 1SR

www.barringtonstoke.co.uk

Front cover image: Bathing at La Grenouillère (1869) by
Claude Monet

ISBN 1-84299-179-5

Edited by Julia Rowlandson
Cover design by Helen Ferguson
Picture research by Kate MacPhee

Designed and typeset by GreenGate Publishing Services,
Tonbridge
Printed in Great Britain by The Bath Press

Barrington Stoke acknowledge support from the Scottish Arts
Council towards the publication of this title.

Scottish
Arts Council
LOTTERY FUNDED

Contents

Introduction

In 1874 a group of artists took the unusual step of organising an art exhibition of their own paintings. They were fed up because the judges of the most important art exhibition in Paris, which took place at the Salon every year, had turned them all down. They thought that the judges were too old-fashioned in their views on art to value their work. Among this group were the artists **Monet**, **Renoir**, **Sisley**, **Pissarro**, **Degas**, **Cézanne**, **Morisot** and **Boudin**. They are now famous artists but in the 1870s their work was often not understood and was even laughed at.

Their own independent exhibition opened on 15th April, 1874. Among the 12 pieces of work put on show by **Claude Monet** was a painting of the sea called **Impression – Sunrise**. He had finished it two years before in 1872 and used the term *impression* to describe the free way in which he had painted it.

Impression – Sunrise (1872) by Claude Monet
Musée Marmottan, Paris, France

PART ONE

Many of the visitors to the exhibition were shocked by the work they saw. The critic, **Louis Leroy**, wrote a nasty review in a magazine called *Le Charivari*. He made fun of the artists' work and meant to insult them by calling his article *Exhibition of the Impressionists*. He said that wallpaper in the first stages of its design was more complete than Monet's painting!

The word 'Impressionists' was meant to poke fun at the work of these artists but it stuck with them. Impressionism became the term given to this new direction in art that took place in the late 1860s to early 1880s. The paintings are now very famous and well-loved all over the world.

In order to understand more about Impressionism we need to find out the answers to the following five questions:

- Where did Impressionism come from?
- What was Impressionism?
- Who were the Impressionists?
- What and who influenced Impressionist artists to work in the way they did?
- What did the Impressionists like to paint and what methods did they use?

Where did Impressionism come from?

The Movement of **Impressionism** came about mainly as a response to two things. One was the development of a new approach to painting from nature and the other was a reaction against the *traditional* methods used to judge art by the Royal Academy.

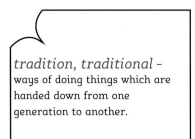

tradition, traditional – ways of doing things which are handed down from one generation to another.

Reaction against the Academy

The Royal Academy of Painting and Sculpture had strict control over the training of artists. There were rules on how to paint and lectures were given on what sort of techniques and subjects would be accepted. Young artists were taught how to bring some expression into their work without moving too far away from the old ways of doing things. Those artists who kept to the rules were often rewarded by having their work displayed by the judges in the famous yearly exhibition at the Salon. On average, about 400,000 people visited this show each year and it had the power to make or break an artist's career. If a young artist's work was seen there, his future as a painter was more or less guaranteed.

For the Academy, the subject matter of the paintings was very important. Some subjects were thought to be more suitable for art.

History painting was ranked first, large paintings about Ancient Greek and Roman myths, famous events in history or stories from the Bible. To be successful, painters had to spend much of their time making painstaking studies from the old masters of several hundred years before.

Portraiture was ranked second, but only portraits of famous or rich people were allowed. After this, came the painting of animals and then came Landscape and Still Life painting.

If any artist dared to go against the standards of the Academy he was refused entry to the Salon exhibition. Artists became more and more fed up and began to protest against what the Salon judges said. When thousands of works were rejected by the Salon in 1863, there were so many complaints that the French Emperor said they must organise another exhibition for all the paintings that had been refused. This was called the Salon des Refusés.

Impressionism

Many of the painters, who were later known as the Impressionists, had their work rejected by the Salon. They decided to challenge the ideas and judgements of the Academy and set up their own exhibition in which they could choose the paintings they wanted to show themselves.

In 1874, the famous photographer, Felix Tournachon, known as Nadar, lent them studios in a smart area of Paris for their first independent exhibition. From this time, the name 'Impressionists' stuck to this group of artists. In total, there were eight 'Impressionist' exhibitions, the last one being in 1886.

Developments in landscape painting

The Academy accepted landscape paintings that were carefully arranged and not wild or natural looking; landscapes with old temple ruins in them which showed scenes from history or mythology. Although painters did make quick sketches of the countryside, they only used these sketches in their studios as studies for their paintings of nature, which they planned with great thought.

Hampstead Heath (1821) by John Constable
Private Collection

During the early part of the 19th century painters became more and more interested in showing nature as it really was. In England, **John Constable** began making accurate studies of changes in the weather and recorded cloud formations at different times of the day. (**Hampstead Heath**, 1821)

During the 1840s in France, a group of painters (who were later to be called the Barbizon School) set up near the village of Barbizon in the Forest of Fontainbleau, south of Paris. They worked outside in the open air (*en plein air*) and tried to paint nature as it was. Amongst these artists were **Camille Corot (The Gust of Wind**, 1867) and **Charles Daubigny**. Daubigny was one of the first to think that the sketches he made outside were finished enough to put into exhibitions.

The Gust of Wind (1867) by Camille Corot
Pushkin Museum, Moscow, Russia

At the same time, other artists such as **Johan Jongkind** (**Entrance of the Port of Honfleur**, 1864) and **Eugene Boudin** (**Boats at Low Tide on the Estuary at Trouville**, 1864) were producing sea and beach scenes on the Normandy coast. All these paintings were fresh and immediate unlike the more planned landscapes that the Academy liked better.

These artists were a big influence on the younger artists. From 1863 on, **Monet, Renoir, Sisley** and **Bazille** (**Landscape at Chailly**, 1865) often took the hour-long train journey from Paris to the Forest of Fontainbleau to make their own sketches straight from nature. It was here that they began to develop the techniques and ideas which we recognise as Impressionist art.

What was Impressionism?

'Impressionism' was the name given to an art movement in the 1860s to 1880s. Its main aim was to paint the modern world as it was, in a way which would show everyday scenes as important events. They shocked the old established artists of the Academy and the Ecole des Beaux-Arts in Paris by their daring *compositions*, sketchy painting methods and bright colours.

The Impressionists were inspired by the poet and art critic, **Charles Baudelaire**, to make paintings which showed the 'heroism of modern life'. Their subjects included Parisian streets, café nightlife, leisure resorts, train stations, picnics in the park and gardens, behind the scenes at the ballet, theatres, horse racing, river and beach scenes, country and industrialised landscapes, and more private scenes inside the home.

composition – arrangement of the parts of a picture.

conventions – rules, set ways of doing things.

tradition, traditional – ways of doing things which are handed down from one generation to another.

Their experiments in colour, style and *composition* challenged the *conventions* of *traditional* art and changed the way we see the world around us. They influenced not only the next generation of painters including **Paul Gauguin** and **Vincent Van Gogh** but paved the way for many of the great masters of colour in the 20th century.

Who were the Impressionists?

Although today we recognise 'Impressionist' artists by their vivid sense of light and atmosphere, they were at the time a group of artists who had their own careers and whose aims and styles were different. They were shocking because they chose to paint subjects which did not fit in with the 'grand art of painting'. The Royal Academy of Art in Paris wanted painting to consist of idealised scenes with moral lessons, not quick sketches of everyday life and popular leisure spots.

These artists did not set out to begin a new art movement called 'Impressionism'. In fact, their first group exhibition in 1874 was called simply, *Painters, sculptors, engravers, etc. Inc.* The most important thing these artists shared was their wish to show work using techniques and styles that they had chosen. They also wanted to paint subjects which were relevant to modern life.

The main 'Impressionist' artists were

Edouard **Manet** (1832–1883)   Claude **Monet** (1840–1926)

Camille **Pissarro** (1830–1903)   Edgar **Degas** (1834–1917)

Pierre-Auguste **Renoir** (1841–1919)   Berthe **Morisot** (1841–1895)

Mary **Cassatt** (1845–1926)   Alfred **Sisley** (1839–1899)

Gustave **Caillebotte** (1848–1894)   Paul **Cézanne** (1839–1906)

During the 1860s many of these artists met to discuss their ideas in the Café Guerbois in the Batignolles area of Paris. They were often joined by art critics and writers, such as Emile Zola, who shocked readers by writing about exactly how things were in his novels. They argued about the way art and writing should go. They had strong opinions and on one occasion **Manet** challenged the art critic, Edmond Duranty, to a duel! Duranty was wounded but the two men settled their differences and became friends again.

Although life was exciting for these young artists they were very poor for many years. **Manet**, **Caillebotte** and **Morisot** were rich enough to give some support to the others, but the Impressionist paintings were hard to sell and so at first, they made little money.

In the end, buyers and patrons came along who valued their work. The most famous of these was a man called Paul Durand-Ruel (1831–1922), who started buying their paintings in the 1870s. Later, in 1886, he took their work to America where rich business people collected it. It was only then, 20 years after their first experiments, that these young artists got some regular money and professional success.

What and who influenced Impressionist artists to work in the way they did?

The influence of social and economic changes in France

The Impressionists lived in a time of great social and economic change in Europe. Britain and France were becoming industrial powers. The population of cities was growing fast and factories gave work to many people who left the countryside for the towns. Paris underwent great change during the years 1850–1870.

In 1848, many people were fed up with their living and working conditions and the way countries were ruled and governed. Revolution swept Europe but failed. In 1852, Napoleon III, Napoleon Bonaparte's nephew, came to power in France. He set up the Second Empire and began to modernise and reshape Paris.

Impressionism

Napoleon III told his architect, Baron Haussmann, to redesign the old areas of Paris in which most of the poor and working people lived. Much of the old medieval city of Paris was destroyed to make way for wide boulevards (streets) and expensive shops and apartments. Over 350,000 working people were thrown out of their homes in old Paris and went to live on the edge of the city. Paris was changed forever and the richer middle classes moved into Haussmann's elegant new buildings and visited the newly built theatres, cafés, restaurants and parks. We can see this new Paris in **Manet's Music in the Tuileries Gardens**, 1862, and in many Impressionist paintings, such as **Caillebotte's Rue de Paris: A Rainy Day**, 1877. It was these paintings of everyday life in the new Paris that caused so many arguments in the art world of the 1860s and 1870s.

Music in the Tuileries Gardens (1862) by Edouard Manet
National Gallery, London, UK

Rue de Paris: A Rainy Day (1877) by Gustave Caillebotte
Musée Marmottan, Paris, France

The influence of Edouard Manet and Gustave Courbet

The Impressionists were not the first artists to challenge the old-fashioned and *traditional* standards of art. Painters such as **Gustave Courbet** and **Edouard Manet** had already rebelled against the strict rules of the Academy. In the 1860s, both these artists organised their own exhibitions after the Salon judges had insulted and rejected their work.

Gustave Courbet and his 'Manifesto of Realism'

As early as 1846, the French poet and art critic Charles Baudelaire called upon artists to make paintings which expressed 'the heroism of modern life'. What he meant by this was that he wanted to see ordinary people in everyday settings and not just famous figures from history or the Bible.

The Stone Breakers (1849) by Gustave Courbet
Gemaeldegalerie Alte Meister, Dresden, Germany

socialist – someone who believes that the community should organise the production of wealth and how it should be spent.

manifesto – document which sets out the main aims of a group of artists.

At the time, **Gustave Courbet** was one of the few artists who took up this challenge. He thought that an artist should rely on his own direct experience of things and said, 'I cannot paint an angel because I have never seen one'. In 1849, the year after the Revolution, he exhibited his painting called **The Stone Breakers**. It caused bitter arguments because it showed two workers in such a realistic and matter-of-fact way. Their work was hard and heavy, breaking stones by hand for long hours every day. Courbet was a *socialist* and felt sorry for working people. He showed the old man and boy with a lot of dignity in their backbreaking work.

In 1855, the judges at the Salon turned down Courbet. He was so angry that he organised his own exhibition in a large wooden shed nearby. He also wrote and handed out his '*Manifesto* of Realism' which explained why he thought it was so important to paint exactly what he saw.

Edouard Manet and the painting of modern life

Edouard Manet also led the way to a new style of painting using modern subjects. He too, was a friend of the poet Charles Baudelaire who wrote a long essay in 1859 called *The Painter of Modern Life*. In it he called upon artists to portray present-day life and show people 'how great and poetic we are in our patent leather shoes and our neckties'.

Both Manet and Baudelaire admired the work of **Constantin Guys**. Guys did quick pen and ink sketches of everyday scenes of people around Paris, for popular magazines and newspapers. Baudelaire said that an artist should be a '*flâneur*' or somebody who roamed the city observing the *anonymous* crowds.

In 1862 Manet put in a portrait of Baudelaire in his painting **Music in the Tuileries Gardens** (see page 12). It is a picture of Manet's family with his writer and artist friends having a day out in the park. Many critics thought it was a terrible picture because Manet had just painted an everyday leisure scene and had not followed many of the rules of picture making. On purpose, Manet had constructed it in a new and challenging way.

First of all, he did not draw the scene using *perspective* so the viewer is not taken into the picture to one focus point. Instead, his friends are painted in a large block which stretches across the front of the painting. Some of the figures are cut off at the edge of the picture making it look like a careless *snapshot* and not a carefully constructed group portrait.

Manet also tried out different ways of using paint. Instead of using the old method of building up tones and not showing any brushstrokes, Manet created a pattern of dark and light areas across the picture. He also sketched in faces with only a few dashes of paint. This gave an instant and sketchy feeling to the picture.

flâneur – a person who strolls about observing people.

anonymous – nameless and unknown.

perspective – a way of constructing a picture from a particular viewpoint as though you were looking through a window into it.

snapshot – natural looking photograph taken quickly.

Manet's paintings caused a sensation when they were shown to the public. He often took *traditional* and *classical* subjects and reworked them in a modern way. In 1863, his paintings, **Olympia** and **Le Déjeuner sur l'Herbe** caused huge scandals because they were not idealised nudes in correct poses against backgrounds from the Myths. Many art critics were offended by his work and wrote nasty articles about him but Manet inspired many of the Impressionist painters such as **Edgar Degas** and **Berthe Morisot** to try out new styles and subjects.

The influence of other countries and cultures

In 1855, 1867 and 1878 three huge 'Universal Exhibitions' were organised in Paris. They displayed artwork and objects from around the world. These exhibitions were very popular. Artists found out that a lot of the work from other cultural backgrounds did not follow the same rules as the Academy taught them.

The Impressionist group of artists was fascinated by Japanese art. During the 1850s many Japanese things were brought into France including clothes, screens, fans and prints. Artists began to collect these prints and loved the way the Japanese artists used flat areas of colour and different ways to create a sense of space without using *perspective*. **Degas** and **Caillebotte** began to use unusual viewpoints and **Manet** and **Monet** began to flatten their colour work and to make it simpler.

Le Déjeuner sur l'Herbe (1863) by Edouard Manet
Musée d'Orsay, Paris, France

The Rehearsal (1874) by Edgar Degas
Fogg Art Museum, Harvard University Art Museums, USA, Bequest from the Collection of Maurice Wertheim, Class 1906

The influence of new technology

The invention of the camera and photography

Many of the Impressionist artists were influenced by the new art of photography. Degas described a photograph as, 'an image of magical instantaneity' and captured the same sense of *immediacy* in his paintings of the Ballet. In **The Rehearsal** of 1874, (see page 15) Degas created a *snapshot* effect in the way the dancers were blurred and the figures at the front right were cut off by the frame of the painting.

The Impressionists knew about the work of the famous photographer, Nadar. Degas and Monet in particular, loved the *immediacy* of photography. Monet owned four cameras in the 1880s and Degas bought one of the new Kodak *snapshot* cameras in 1896. From 1878 on, Degas was very interested in experiments by the photographer Eadweard Muybridge in capturing movement. Muybridge published his findings in a book called *Animal Locomotion* in 1887. In it he showed sequences of movements by animals and people.

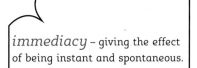

immediacy – giving the effect of being instant and spontaneous.

Animal Locomotion (1887) by Eadweard Muybridge
Hulton-Deutsch Collection/CORBIS

Artists' equipment

Changes in artists' equipment were happening which made it much easier to paint outdoors. Lightweight easels and metal tubes for paint came on to the market, which meant that painters could carry their equipment and materials easily into the countryside and onto the beach. Impressionist painters wanted to work directly from their subjects and the heavy old studio easels were not suitable.

Also, there was a wide range of new paint colours being manufactured. You could now get bright colours such as chromium yellow and cobalt violet. In the past, painters had painted on dark backgrounds using a lot of earth colours, browns and dull reds. The Impressionists wanted to capture the effects of light and the brilliant colours in nature, so they worked on white backgrounds with dashes of bright colour straight from the tube.

complementary colours – colours opposite each other in the colour wheel which create a vibrant effect when placed near to one another. These 'complementary' colours include red/green, yellow/purple and blue/orange.

vibrant – vivid, thrilling.

Theories of colour

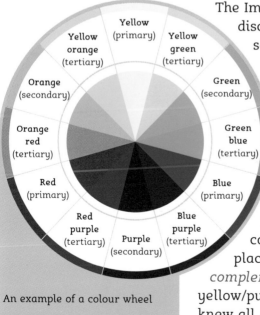

An example of a colour wheel

The Impressionists were also influenced by scientific discoveries about the effects of colour. The scientist, Eugene Chevreul, published his findings in 1839 in a book called *On the Law of Simultaneous Contrast of Colours.*

Chevreul constructed a colour wheel with warm colours (red, orange, yellow) on one side and cool colours (purple, blue, green) on the other (Chevreul's Colour Circle). He explained how we saw colours differently depending on which colour they were seen next to. Colours opposite each other in the colour wheel created a *vibrant* effect when placed near to one another. These *complementary colours* included red/green, yellow/purple and blue/orange. The Impressionists knew all about these effects and used *complementary colours* in shadows instead of blacks and greys. Monet produced stunning effects using these methods in his painting **Boats; Regatta at Argenteuil**, 1872 (page 22).

What did the Impressionists like to paint and what methods did they use?

The Impressionist artists shared many aims, but they also developed their own techniques. Each of them had favourite subjects and their own way of capturing *fleeting* moments and *shimmering* light effects on their canvases.

Impressionist painters used the new vivid colours on white canvases to create brilliant effects of light. They also understood the latest scientific research on colour and experimented with its effects.

Edouard Manet (1832–1883)

- Shocked the Salon with his paintings of nudes in modern settings and informal portraits of family and friends.
- His interest in photography and Japanese prints led him to try out new *compositions*.
- Experimented with strong contrasts in tone to create an overall patterned effect in paintings like **Music in the Tuileries Gardens**, 1862 (see page 12).
- Produced paintings of glimpses of café life in blurred and quick brushstrokes (**Waitress Serving Beer**, 1878–1879).

Waitress Serving Beer (1878–1879) by Edouard Manet
Musée d'Orsay, Paris, France

Pierre-Auguste Renoir (1841–1919)

- Started as a porcelain painter and learnt how to use pure colours on a light background for vivid effects.
- His palette was made up of *vibrant* colours: lead white, vermilion, emerald green, cobalt blue and Naples yellow.
- Early on, he studied landscape painting but loved painting people most and was skilled at portraits.
- Was a master at creating the effects of dappled sunlight and movement as well as the delicate pearly tones of people's faces and hands (see **The Swing**, 1876 on page 36).

Woman and Child in a Garden at Bougival (1882) by Berthe Morisot
National Gallery of Scotland, Edinburgh, Scotland

Berthe Morisot (1841–1895)

- In her early paintings she was influenced by the landscape artist, Corot, and later by the techniques of Edouard Manet.

- By the 1870s she had developed her own distinctive style. Paintings such as **Woman and Child in a Garden at Bougival**, 1882, show her free brushwork and flickering light effects.

- She built up her pictures with swift slashes of colour over the whole canvas. Details and outlines are smeared and blurred. Morisot smudged areas and wiped and blotted her paints. In this way she created a *luminous* effect of light and movement.

- One art critic, who loved her brushwork and subtle colour *harmonies*, said, 'She grinds flower petals on to her palette so as to spread them later on her canvas, with airy, witty touches, thrown down almost haphazardly'.

luminous – glowing with light.

harmony, harmonies, harmonious – being in agreement, peaceful, not contrasting or jarring.

19

Edgar Degas (1834–1917)

- Combined his superb drawing skills with the Impressionists' aim to capture light effects, atmosphere and the immediate moment.
- His favourite subjects were café nightlife, the ballet, horse-racing and studies of women at work or relaxing.
- Often chose unusual viewpoints in his paintings. The *snapshot* effects of photography and the designs in Japanese woodcuts, which were very popular at the time, influenced him. He liked the way figures were often cropped (cut) in both photos and prints, and included this in his paintings. See Mary Cassatt at the Louvre, 1885.

Mary Cassatt at the Louvre (1885) by Edgar Degas
Rosenwald Collection

Mary Cassatt (1844–1926)

- Was born in America but came to live in France in 1866. Was very *influenced* by the work of Degas and was famous for portraying the everyday lives of women – having tea, reading the newspaper, driving a horse and carriage or watching a play at the theatre.
- Produced some excellent portraits such as that of her mother called **Reading Le Figaro**, 1883.
- Loved Japanese prints and was a keen printmaker herself. Cassatt, Degas and Pissarro showed their prints at the fifth Impressionist Exhibition in 1880. In 1891, Cassatt completed 25 sets of 10 prints. They were based around the tasks women did at home and they used Japanese print methods (**The Coiffure**, 1891).

Reading Le Figaro (1883) by Mary Cassatt
Private Collection

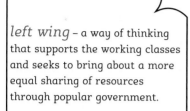

left wing – a way of thinking that supports the working classes and seeks to bring about a more equal sharing of resources through popular government.

Camille Pissarro (1830–1903)

- Was born about 10 years before Monet, Renoir and Sisley and seemed to be almost a father figure to the Impressionist group.

- Was influenced by the landscape painter, Corot, but always preferred to include figures in his own paintings of the countryside. He was the most *left wing* and politically active of the Impressionists and was always interested in the daily lives of working people.

- Usually painted peasant girls at rest or working in the fields (see **Peasants Guarding their Cows**, 1882). Degas called them 'angels who go to market'.

- Painted with broad brushstrokes and filled his pictures with colour and light.

Paul Cézanne (1839–1906)

- In his early career, Cézanne worked in an Impressionist style but he later he became famous as a Post-Impressionist artist.

- His use of colour, space and form influenced the later generations of painters a lot and he is now thought of as the father of Cubism and abstract art.

- His paintings in the 1870s were influenced by the work of Pissarro. Paintings like **Dr. Gachet's House at Auvers**, 1873, show his use of subtle colour *harmonies* and effects of light.

Dr. Gachet's House at Auvers (1873) by Paul Cézanne
Musée d'Orsay, Paris, France

21

Boats; Regatta at Argenteuil (1872) by Claude Monet
Musée d'Orsay, Paris, France

Claude Monet (1840–1926)

- Was good at using strong colour contrasts in his paintings and became well-known for his method of putting paint on in swift dashes and slabs of colour. (see **Boats; Regatta at Argenteuil**, 1872)
- Was really fascinated by the effects of light on water and on moisture in the atmosphere.
- Painted steam from trains, heat hazes and sunlight on the River Seine, mist and fog over the River Thames and the Houses of Parliament in London, and sunlight reflected on the lily pond in his much loved garden at Giverny. Reflections of clouds and plants in the water create a *shimmering* surface of light.

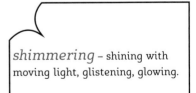

shimmering – shining with moving light, glistening, glowing.

Floods at Port-Marly (1876) by
Alfred Sisley

Musée d'Orsay, Paris, France

Alfred Sisley (1839–1899)

- Concentrated mostly on river scenes around the villages on the River Seine, west of Paris. Liked ordinary scenes with working people in them.

- Was influenced by English landscape painters such as **Turner** and **Constable** and the French Barbizon group of painters such as **Corot**.

- In the late 1860s and 1870s, he found his own Impressionist style and kept to these techniques for the rest of his life.

- Was fascinated by seasonal changes and different weather conditions.

- His series of paintings of the floods at Port-Marly show warm and cool colour contrasts in the cloudy sky which are reflected in dashes of turquoise blues and oranges on the water's surface. (See **Floods at Port-Marly**, 1876.)

- He was most well known for his free brushwork which allowed him to create movement and light in expansive skies and create a beautiful sense of natural light throughout his landscapes.

The Floor Scrapers (1875) by Gustave Caillebotte
Musée d'Orsay, Paris, France

Gustave Caillebotte (1848–1894)

- Although Caillebotte did not use the Impressionist techniques of bright colours and swift brushwork, he created strikingly modern images of the new Paris streets. His painting called **Paris, a Rainy Day,** 1876–1877 caused a sensation at the third Impressionist Exhibition in 1877 (see page 12).

- Used cleverly worked out compositions and distorted *perspectives*.

- Also imitated the effects of photography by cropping people at the edge of his paintings for a *snapshot* effect of life as it is.

- One of the few artists to paint pictures of working men. He uses a steep view of the floor in his painting called **The Floor Scrapers** of 1875.

perspective – a way of constructing a picture from a particular viewpoint as though you were looking through a window into it.

Biographies of Artists and their Paintings Explored

PART TWO

Self-portrait (1855) by Edgar Degas
Musée d'Orsay, Paris, France

Born: 19th July 1834
Died: 27th September 1917
Place of Birth: Paris
Family details: His father ran a private bank in Paris and Naples. He was the eldest of five children.
Paintings analysed:
The Absinth Drinker, 1875–1876
The Star, 1876–1877

EDGAR DEGAS

The Cotton Exchange in New Orleans (1873) by Edgar Degas
Musée des Beaux-Arts, Pau, France

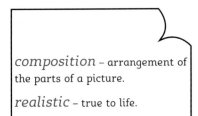

composition – arrangement of the parts of a picture.

realistic – true to life.

Edgar Degas' father came from an aristocratic Italian background. His mother was of *Creole* descent from New Orleans in USA. He was the eldest son of five children.

In 1853, when Degas was 19, he began studying law but gave it up after less than a year to become an artist. His self-portrait of 1855 shows him as a smartly dressed and determined middle class young man.

Although Degas was a student at the studio of Louis Lamothe, he was largely self-taught. He spent much of his time in the Louvre copying the paintings of great artists such as **Ingres** and then in 1856 travelled to Italy to go on with his studies. He returned to Paris in 1859 and in 1862 came under the influence of **Edouard Manet's** ideas on modern art.

Degas served in the National Guard during the Franco-Prussian War. Afterwards, in 1872, he visited New Orleans, USA, where he had relatives in the cotton trade. **The Cotton Exchange in New Orleans**, 1873, shows the influence of Manet in its *composition* and use of black and white. The cropping of the man on the left and the casual arrangement of figures shows Degas' interest in *snapshot* photography and *realistic* effects.

When Degas returned to Paris he helped to set up the first Impressionist Exhibition in 1874 but later showed 24 of his paintings in the second exhibition. His father had died a year earlier and, in 1876, Degas found out his brother, René, had run the family business so badly that they were almost bankrupt. Degas was set on paying off all debts by selling his paintings. Luckily, in 1878, his painting of **The Cotton Exchange** was bought by the Museum of Pau in Southern France for 2000 francs.

Degas never liked painting in the open air. He preferred to paint the stunning effects of artificial light, so he visited music halls, cafés at night, concerts and circuses (see **Aux Ambassadeurs**, 1877). This was an open-air café on the Boulevard Champs Elysees where Degas made paintings of his favourite singer, Emilie Becat. The stage is seen from within the audience. We look over the heads of the musicians at the performer's faces which are lit from beneath. Over half of his life's work was based on paintings of the ballet, both on stage and behind the scenes in rehearsals (see page 15, **The Rehearsal**, 1874).

Degas loved to show the effects of movement in his pictures. He admired the work of the photographers Nadar, and Eadweard Muybridge who published a book of photographs called *Animal Locomotion* (see page 16). These photos inspired Degas' bronze sculptures of ballet dancers, and jumping horses. In 1881 Degas exhibited his realistic sculpture of the **Little Dancer aged Fourteen Years**. His model was the Belgian ballerina **Marie Van Goettan**. The sculpture was one metre tall and had real hair and wore a real ballet dress and shoes. Some critics thought the sculpture was ugly because it was too *naturalistic* and not *idealised*. **Arabesque Penchée**, 1885–1890 (see page 29) also showed his close study of movement.

Little Dancer aged Fourteen Years (1881) by Edgar Degas
Private Collection

Aux Ambassadeurs (1877) by Edgar Degas
Musée des Beaux Arts Lyons

naturalistic – realistic method that attempts to portray nature truthfully.

idealised – something which is idealised is shown as the perfect model rather than how it really is.

Arabesque Penchée (1885–1890) by
Edgar Degas
Hirschhorn Museum, Washington

Degas enjoyed working in different media and materials. In the fourth Impressionist Exhibition of 1879 he exhibited works in pastel chalks and on painted fans. He was a fine *draughtsman* who enjoyed drawing the human figure. In the 1880s he completed a series of paintings and pastels of women relaxing, bathing and at work. **Women Ironing**, 1884–1886, and **The Tub**, 1886, are good examples.

Sadly, by 1901, Degas was nearly blind and worked mainly on large canvases with broad strokes of chalk. He did produce landscape drawings in pastels but these were from memory and not *en plein air* (in the open air). They are poetic and colourful visions rather than *realistic* studies.

During his lifetime he had two solo exhibitions and took part in many group exhibitions. A large collection of his work, The Cammondo collection, was given to the Louvre at the outbreak of World War 1 in 1914.

In September 1917 Degas died at the age of 83. After his death, about 150 wax figures were found in his studio and many were later made into bronze statuettes. Degas had probably turned to sculpture when his sight failed him. Today, he is one of the best known of the Impressionist group of painters and his work is exhibited all over the world.

Women Ironing (1884–1886)
by Edgar Degas
Musée d'Orsay, Paris

draughtsman – someone who is able to draw well.

The Absinth Drinker, 1875–1876, by Edgar Degas

Musée d'Orsay, Paris

Ideas
- Compare this painting with those of the American artist, Edward Hopper (1882–1967). Hopper's favourite subject was *alienation* and he often painted lonely people sitting in cafés in big American cities.
- Try painting the effect of greyish wintry light on clothes and reflected light on other objects.
- Make studies of peoples' faces when they are lost in thought or daydreaming.

Background

Degas loved to watch life in the 'new' Paris. Many cafés put on entertainment and the Impressionists often painted popular performers and the crowds watching them. Paintings like Degas' **Aux Ambassadeurs**, 1877 (see page 28) show people enjoying the city's crowded nightspots.

However, crowds can also be anonymous and indifferent. People often feel *isolated* and lonely in large cities. The poet Baudelaire had written that many of the heroes of modern life were in fact the homeless poor and the painter Edouard Manet had already made them the subject of paintings such as **The Old Musician**, 1862, and **The Ragpicker**, 1869. In 1876 Degas completed **The Absinth Drinker** which showed a sadder and more lonely side to café life.

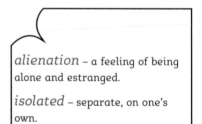

alienation – a feeling of being alone and estranged.

isolated – separate, on one's own.

Absinth was a popular drink but one that had terrible effects for those who became addicted to it. Degas' painting was done in the same year as his friend, the writer Emile Zola, published his Realist novel called *L'Assommoir* (*The Laundress*). Zola told the sad story of a *laundress* who sank slowly into poverty and alcoholism, and her daughter who became a prostitute. Both the painting and the book caused many arguments. People were shocked when faced with the misery of some people's lives.

Content

The way this picture has been constructed is, as though we, the viewers, are actually sitting in the same café just across from the unhappy couple. Out of the corner of our eye we see that the woman is drinking Absinth and the man has a hangover remedy called 'mazagran'.

The woman stares down in front of her, lost in her own private thoughts. Her friend leans forward on his arm and gazes hopelessly away from her. Their reflections in the mirror behind them make the fact they are separate and lonely more obvious.

They are both shabbily dressed. The woman's shoulders are slumped and her feet are stretched out in front of her as though she expects to be sitting in the same place for hours. The man is also slumped forward. He has a resigned and fed-up expression on his face as he puffs away at his pipe.

The couple in Degas' painting was not in fact a pair of real down-and-outs but was modelled by two of his friends. The woman was a well-known actress called Ellen Andrée who posed for several of the other Impressionists including Renoir and Manet. She seems a lot happier in Manet's **At the Café** of 1878. The man in Degas' **The Absinth Drinker** is the artist and engraver, Marcellin Desboutin.

Form

Degas makes the viewer into a casual observer but also makes us feel very sorry for the couple. Our eyes go straight to the downcast woman, but at the same time, we are kept separate from her by the large space between the tables in the *foreground* of the painting.

Degas has left out the legs of the tables on purpose so that our eye skims across the zigzag shapes of empty tables, straight to the unhappy couple. The marble slabs of the table-tops seem to hover in mid-air and this causes a sense of tension and makes things seem uncertain and unfixed. This increases our own uneasy feelings about the lives of this miserable pair. Their unhappiness touches our own lives and yet we are still outsiders looking on.

The colours in this painting are mostly drab browns and greys. The dull surroundings echo the loneliness and *alienation* of its customers.

Process

Degas uses quick brushstrokes and pale colours to describe the cold, marble table-tops.

The lace curtains hanging in the café windows are reflected in the mirror behind the couple. A greyish light comes through the windows and falls on the woman's hat and jacket and catches the man's face and shirt. Degas has skilfully captured this effect of light with a few quick dashes of white and pale grey paint.

Degas sketched in the woman's skirt with areas of reddy-brown paint on black. He described the texture of the lacy bows on her shoes with thick, white paint. Her face is painted with soft changes of tone. This contrasts with the man's rougher set face which Degas has painted in patches of darker colours.

Mood

Judging by the light in this painting it is either early morning or the afternoon of a dull day. The greyish cold light reflects the depressed mood of the silent drinkers.

The couple has an air of hopelessness and loneliness about them. Both are locked into their own separate worlds and they appear to have nothing left to say to each other.

The Star (L'Etoile), 1876–1877, by Edgar Degas

Musée d'Orsay, Paris

Ideas
- Try drawing a friend's face when it is lit from underneath by an anglepoise lamp. Use chalk pastels on grey paper to create different light effects.

- Make some quick charcoal drawings of a figure in movement. Ask your model to hold different positions for about five minutes each while you make a quick sketch of the main lines of the pose.

- Make a visit to a ballet performance and try sketching some of the dancers.

Background

Most of the Impressionist painters loved to paint outside and record the effects of natural light. Edgar Degas was different, the effects of artificial light fascinated him and most of his paintings were done inside theatres, cafés, workplaces and homes.

He really loved the ballet. From the 1870s he completed many studies of the ballerinas at the Paris Opera in rehearsal, at rest and on stage. He used charcoal, pastels and oil paints.

Degas was fascinated by the ability of photography to capture movement and admired the experiments of Eadweard Muybridge in recording sequences of animal and human movements (see page 16). Degas had known Muybridge's work since 1878 but it was after the publication of Muybridge's book called *Animal Locomotion* in 1887 that Degas produced most of his wax figures of ballerinas and horses in various *dynamic* poses.

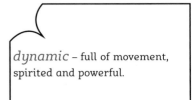

dynamic – full of movement, spirited and powerful.

Content

This view of the stage was drawn from one of the front boxes at the Paris Opera House. These boxes were very expensive and gave close-up views of the performance. Three of these front boxes were used by the French Emperor himself.

Degas often drew the stage from this angle and in **At the Ballet, Woman with a Fan**, 1883–1885, we can see the stage from behind another spectator in one of these boxes.

The star of the ballet dances into the right-hand corner of the picture leaving much of the stage empty. Our gaze is focussed just on her and she appears to be looking at us.

In the background amongst the sketchily drawn dancers, Degas has put in the figure of a man in a black suit. These men often appear in his paintings of the ballet such as **The Curtain**, 1880, where small groups of men wait at the back of the stage and in the wings. These men paid for the most expensive boxes at the Opera and this gave them the right to go backstage to see and meet the dancers.

Process

Degas used bold sketchy brushstrokes for the scenery in the background. His swift handling of the paint produces blurred sketches of the other dancers on the stage. This blurring of details adds to the *snapshot* effect of a single moment in the performance.

The main dancer floats like a butterfly in a pale greyish green area. Highlights on her face and body are painted in pale pink while the shadows are in greyish-green tones like the stage floor. This makes her look transparent and creates her as a vision of lightness and grace – a true star!

The star ballerina is lit from underneath. Light shines under her chin, arms and chest and falls more fully on the one fragile leg she is standing on. Degas uses a few confident, strokes of paint to create the dancer's leg. He shows his clear understanding of *anatomy* and his superb drawing skills in drawing the foreshortened view of the ballerina from above.

To create a magical glow of light on the thin layers of the ballerina's skirt, Degas drags dry white paint across the surface of the grey painted stage. He uses a few touches of red paint for the flowers on her dress.

Form

Degas has drawn a diagonal composition across the picture which makes the dancer's movement more *dynamic* and exciting. It also gives the effect of a snapshot photograph.

This diagonal composition was also influenced by Degas' love of Japanese prints. He admired the way Japanese artists often constructed their pictures like this and left a lot of space with empty, flat areas of colour.

Sketches of other dancers hidden in the scenery create another strong diagonal at the top of the painting. Degas drew the ballerina's outstretched arms on a diagonal too. One arm reaches out towards us and the other joins up visually to the background.

Mood

This painting creates the magical atmosphere of a night at the Paris Opera. Degas captures a dramatic moment in the star's performance.

He creates a *dynamic* sense of movement by his sketchy light brushstrokes and quick touches of paint.

Pierre-Auguste Renoir (1867) by
Jean-Frederic Bazille
Musée d'Orsay, Paris

Born: 25th February 1841
Died: 3rd December 1919
Place of Birth: Limoges, South West France
Family details: His father was a tailor. He was the youngest of five children.
Paintings analysed:
The Dance at the Moulin de la Galette, 1876
The Two Sisters, 1881

PIERRE-AUGUSTE RENOIR

When Renoir was five years old his family moved to Paris to find more work. From an early age, he showed a talent for music and art so when he was just 13 he left school and began an apprenticeship as a *porcelain* painter. At the same time, he often went to the Louvre Museum to study the great masters of painting and also took drawing lessons.

By the time he was 19 he had saved enough money to enrol at the studio of Charles Gleyre where he met **Claude Monet**, **Frédéric Bazille** and **Alfred Sisley**. He went on painting trips with them to the Forest of Fontainbleau and met the Barbizon group of landscape artists including **Pissarro**, and **Courbet** (see page 8). When back in Paris, Renoir often went to the Café Guerbois, a favourite meeting place of artists and writers, and there met **Degas** and **Manet** and the novelist, Emile Zola. Bazille painted this portrait of him (page 34) in 1867 which shows an intense young man despite his relaxed pose (**Pierre-August Renoir**, by Jean-Frederic Bazille, 1867).

In 1869, Renoir and Monet spent some time at the resort of La Grenouillère on the banks of the River Seine. This provided the two young artists with what was to become a typical Impressionist subject of people enjoying a day out beside the river in sunny weather. Although Renoir concentrated more than Monet did, on showing the day-trippers in his paintings, both artists were fascinated by the effects of light on the water. They used new kinds of brushstrokes and bright colours to record the sudden and ever-changing effects of light. This was the beginning of Renoir's Impressionist style but his progress was interrupted in 1870 by the Franco-Prussian war during which he served in the army.

Renoir came from a poor background so he depended on the sale of his paintings and the kindness of fellow artists for money. He exhibited his work at many of the eight Impressionist Exhibitions. There he showed one of his most ambitious paintings **The Dance at the Moulin de la Galette**, 1876 (see page 38). In it we can see young people enjoying themselves in an open-air dance in Montmartre, Paris. The effects of dappled sunlight are typical of Renoir's Impressionist style. In the same year, Renoir completed **The Swing**, 1876, again showing people relaxing on a sunny day.

Renoir continued to submit paintings to the Salon jury. He often accepted commissions for portraits and in 1879 he enjoyed success at the Salon with his family portrait of **Madame Charpentier and her children**, 1879. This painting showed the family of the well-known publisher, Georges Charpentier, who helped young artists and introduced them to buyers and collectors.

In 1881, Renoir visited Italy and painted several views of Venice. For a short time his work became more *academic* and *classical* in style but then his dealer, Durand-Ruel, persuaded him to return to his Impressionist style. It was after this that Renoir produced some of his greatest masterpieces including **The Luncheon of the Boating Party**, 1881. Renoir met his future wife Aline Charigot, in 1880 and he painted her, at the front on the left, cuddling a little dog. They had their first son, Pierre, in 1885. They were married in 1890 and four years later had their second son, Jean, who was later to become a famous film director. In 1901 their third son, Claude, was born.

The Swing (1876) by Pierre-Auguste Renoir
Musée d'Orsay, Paris

The Luncheon of the Boating Party (1881) by Pierre-Auguste Renoir
Phillips Collection, Washington DC, USA

Madame Charpentier and her children (1879) by Pierre-Auguste Renoir
Metropolitan Museum of Art, New York, USA

academic – according to the rules of the academy or university.

classical – following the rules of art first established in ancient Greece and Rome.

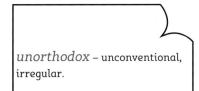

unorthodox – unconventional, irregular.

Renoir refused to take part in the last two Impressionist Exhibitions in 1882 and 1886 because he thought that painters like **Gauguin** and **Pissarro** were becoming too *unorthodox* in their aims. Instead he chose to exhibit in the **International Exhibition** set up by the dealer, Georges Petit. At the same time, his long-standing dealer and collector, Durand-Ruel, exhibited over 300 Impressionist works in a show in New York and 32 were by Renoir. Many of the paintings he completed in the 1880s and 1890s were of women, bathing, dancing, playing music and caring for babies and children.

In 1892, a large exhibition looking back at over a hundred paintings by Renoir was a huge success. Renoir began at last to enjoy financial security and success. Sadly, his health started to become a problem and he suffered from bad arthritis. Painting was his great love and he never gave it up. However, towards the end of his life he had to be carried to his studio and brushes were tied into his hands so he could go on painting.

Renoir had outstanding success in his own lifetime. He had his work shown all around the world including Europe and in America. He became very popular in Germany and was a major influence on the younger generation of painters there.

Renoir lived through World War 1 at his house near Cannes in the South of France. Both his sons were wounded in action and sadly his wife died at the young age of 56 in 1915. Four years later on 3rd December, 1919, Renoir died of pneumonia at the age of 78. Shortly before his death he was invited to see his portrait of the Charpentier family hung in the National Museum of the Louvre in Paris. He had become one of the most famous and highly rated painters in France.

The Dance at the Moulin de la Galette (Bal du Moulin de la Galette), 1876, by Pierre-Auguste Renoir

Private Collection

Background

Today, when we look at Renoir's happy scenes of people at leisure, it is hard to believe how rude his critics were. At the second Impressionist exhibition in 1876, one critic said that Renoir's study of a nude made him think of 'a pile of decomposing flesh' because of the reflected blue tones on the model's skin – **Etude; torse, effet de soleil** (Study; torso, effect of sunlight), 1875.

This painting of working-class people relaxing at an outdoor dance in Montmartre, Paris, was just as badly received when it was shown at the third Impressionist Exhibition in 1877. Critics misunderstood Renoir's use of colour and his light sketchy brushstrokes. One said that there were strange 'purplish clouds' scattered throughout the painting.

His subject of working-class people enjoying themselves was also not accepted as suitable for a fine art painting even though Renoir showed none of the harsh realities of being poor. He wanted to create an idyllic scene of everyone getting on and having fun.

There is none of the social tension we see in Manet's painting of a fashionable public dance, **Masked Ball at the Opera**, 1873. In Manet's picture we see well-off middle-class men in their top hats and suits talking to young working class women in masks and scanty costumes.

Masked Ball at the Opera (1873) by Edouard Manet

Gift of Mrs Horace Havemeyer in memory of her mother-in-law, Louisina W Havemeyer

The Dance at the Moulin de la Galette, 1876, by Pierre-Auguste Renoir

Content

Public dances were popular entertainment in Paris at this time and an old mill on top of Montmartre hill was converted into a café and dance hall. Renoir has chosen to paint a view of the garden courtyard next to the mill which was used by the dancers on hot summer days.

Renoir and his writer and artist friends lived in the Montmartre area of Paris. He has put some of them in the group of people chatting at the front of the picture. They are sitting with local working girls such as shop assistants and laundresses who frequently spent their Sunday afternoons at the dance. Renoir has created an idyllic scene in the dappled sunlight and far from the cares of their often harsh lives.

Renoir's friend and biographer, Georges Rivière, said that Renoir had painted it on the spot but it is more likely that this large painting was drawn up in the studio from many quick sketches.

Process

Renoir started off as a painter of porcelain figurines and loved the pearly colours he could achieve in this craft. The soft skin tones on the women's faces and the light pastel colours used in this painting are inspired by Renoir's knowledge of the delicate effects he had achieved on the white porcelain.

The whole painting is held together by a mixture of the two *complementary* opposites, blue and creamy yellow. The creamy colour of the men's hats and the main dancer's dress stand out well against the blue-grey colour of the ground. Renoir shows the sunlight coming through the overhanging branches with patches of cream and pale mauve across the whole painting.

Renoir has captured a sense of *immediacy* and movement in this picture by the swaying poses of the dancers and the swift feathery brushstrokes. The cropping of the woman talking to the child in the bottom left corner gives a *snapshot* effect as though this is just one instant in the afternoon's entertainment.

Form

Half of the painting is taken up by a group of people talking around a table with drinks on. This group fills a triangular area at the bottom right of the picture. Behind them are the dancers and in the distance we can just make out the musicians on a stage beneath the gas lamps. The dancers become smaller in size the further back they are on the dance floor.

The main focus of the painting is the two young women sitting at the front. Two diagonals in Renoir's *composition* meet on their faces. One diagonal is formed by the dancing couples on the left, the other by the hats of the group on the right.

Renoir links the people together by their easy-going glances at each other. A woman's face can just be seen beside the tree looking towards the young man who has his back towards us in the front of the painting. The dancing couple on the left of the picture also looks across to the main group. In the bottom left corner we just catch sight of a young woman talking to a child. This is how Renoir creates a sense of connection between the people. This is not only his way of bringing together all the different parts of this complex picture but it also creates the feeling of social *harmony* which Renoir wanted to create in his painting.

Mood

Renoir's brother, Edmond, commented that his paintings were the 'most lovely and *harmonious* of the age'. This is very true of the **Dance at the Moulin de la Galette**.

The dappled sunlight creates a mood of joy and movement. Blue and creamy yellows run through the painting creating softened yet vivid colour contrasts.

The smiling groups of people chat and flirt with each other and create a picture of innocent pleasure and friendly company that stays in our memory.

The Two Sisters, 1881, by Pierre-Auguste Renoir

Art Institute of Chicago, IL, USA

Background

This painting is almost life-size and was probably painted at Chatou, a popular riverside resort close to Paris. Chatou was only a few miles south of Argenteuil where Renoir had spent time in the 1870s painting the riverside views with **Monet**.

Renoir did not share Monet's absolute fascination with effects of light in nature and had always been much more interested in painting people. He preferred recording relaxed social events such as **The Rower's Lunch**, 1880, and his famous **Luncheon of the The Boating Party**, 1880–1881 (see page 36). In this picture we can see Renoir's future wife cuddling the dog on the left and the Impressionist painter **Gustave Caillebotte** leaning back on the chair opposite her.

In his painting of **The Two Sisters**, Renoir has combined his interest in boating and riverside scenes with a charming portrait of a young woman with her little sister.

transience, transient – something which is fleeting and does not last.

The Two Sisters, 1881, by Pierre-Auguste Renoir

Form

Renoir has created a bold composition. He has cut the picture in half and divided the foreground from the background with the line of the top of the fence. The sisters sit in a small space in front of this balustrade (fence) and are separated from nature and the countryside that stretches out behind them.

The uprights of the terrace fence are repeated in the vertical lines of the trees growing in the field behind. The older sister is placed right in the middle of the picture and her stunning hat is framed on either side by the vertical lines of the tree trunks.

Highlights of vermilion red take your eye through the painting – from the balls of wool to the hats on the two sisters, the boats in the middle distance and the roof of the house on the far bank of the river. The patches of red contrast well with the different shades of green in the painting and give the painting an exciting brilliance.

Process

Renoir tried to keep his colours as pure as possible so he has mixed his paints straight onto the white canvas. He has not waited for the first layers of paint to dry before adding more *wet-in-wet*. The hands and faces are built up in this way with thin layers of wet paint.

Sometimes Renoir put pure *complementary colours* next to each other to make a stunning effect. The older sister's red hat looks even more vivid because of the green ribbon around it. The balls of wool in the basket on her lap have rich contrasts of colour.

Renoir uses lots of different kinds of brushstrokes to achieve the effects in this painting. He achieves movement and reflections in the river water by dashes of colour diluted with white. The leaves on the trees behind the sisters are stippled in.

The boldest paintwork is on the flowers and wool in the foreground. Here Renoir uses thick paint, pure colours and swift brushstrokes. He captures the curling petals of the flowers and the twists of the wool in single strokes.

Content

A young woman sits on a terrace with her little sister standing beside her. On the older sister's lap there is a basket full of coloured wools, which she may have been winding into balls, or using for knitting or sewing.

Both sisters are young with their lives ahead of them. They have flowers pinned to their hats and clothes and behind them is a field full of early spring blossoms. The trailing plant on the terrace fence is just beginning to shoot young leaves and the trees behind are also showing the first signs of new growth.

Renoir used his knowledge of *porcelain* painting on the young girls' hands and faces. He had learnt this craft when he was a young man and admired the delicate, pure colours on 18th century porcelain statuettes. He also loved paintings by 18th century artists such as Boucher and Watteau because of their pastel shades and pearly effects.

In the distance we can see the river drifting past and the houses and countryside on the far bank. There are people out on the river rowing and the scene reminds us of an earlier painting by Renoir called **Boating on the Seine**, 1879.

Mood

The portrait of the two sisters has a touching quality. The older sister has a sensitive expression which engages with you and the child is appealing because of her young innocence. They are both at the beginning of new phases in their life. The elder sister is just becoming a woman and the younger starting childhood. In the delicate way Renoir has painted them he makes you aware of how fragile life is and how soon the moment passes.

The rich colours and beautiful landscape appeal to our senses. At the same time this is a tranquil scene which makes us contemplate the *transience* of nature and beauty.

Monet in his Floating Studio (1874)
by Edouard Manet
Neue Pinakothek, Munich, Germany

Born: 14th November 1840
Died: 5th December 1926
Place of Birth: Paris
Family details: His father owned a grocery and ship's equipment business. They were middle class.
Paintings analysed:
Bathing at La Grenouillère, 1869
Saint-Lazare Station, 1877
The Waterlily Pond, 1899

CLAUDE MONET

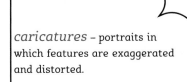

caricatures – portraits in which features are exaggerated and distorted.

When Monet was five years old, the family moved to Le Havre on the Normandy coast. Monet hated school and left when he was just 15 years old. He loved drawing and made money selling *caricatures* of tourists on the local beaches. There he met a local artist called **Eugene Boudin** who encouraged him to paint landscapes straight from nature, *en plein air* (in the open air). Monet said he suddenly realised what painting was all about and that he had a burning desire to become an artist. He persuaded his father to enrol him at a studio workshop in Paris in 1859.

In 1860 he had to do his military service in the French army which held up his artistic studies. He was sent home two years later having caught the serious illness of typhoid. Monet's family did not want him to return to army life and paid for him to study at the Charles Gleyre studio in Paris. It was there that he met other painters like **Renoir**, **Sisley** and **Bazille**. They became strong friends and shared ideas. They went on painting trips to the Forest of Fontainbleau near Paris and learned the techniques of the Barbizon group of landscape painters such as **Corot** and **Pissarro**.

In 1865 Monet had two seascapes accepted by the Salon jury and he was beginning to become known. However, he had little money. He wasn't selling many paintings and his family disapproved so much of his lifestyle that they did not send him money every week. In 1867, Monet's future wife, Camille Doncieux, gave birth to their son but it was hard for the young family who were very poor.

In 1869, he did a lot of painting with Renoir at the holiday resort of La Grenouillère and this was the beginning of the new Impressionist style. In 1870, he married Camille and they spent their honeymoon at Trouville on the Normandy coastline. He painted his young wife on the beach and real grains of sand have been found in the paint (**The Beach at Trouville**, 1870).

Sadly, their happiness was short-lived because the Franco-Prussian War started in 1870. Monet didn't want to be called up to serve in the French army so he fled to London.

The Beach at Trouville (1870) by Claude Monet
National Gallery, London, UK

There he painted a series of views of the Thames and the Houses of Parliament. He studied the work of the famous English artist, **Joseph Turner**, and admired his ability to capture subtle effects of light in paintings such as **Rain, Steam and Speed – The Great Western Railway**, 1844. On his return to France, Monet's fortunes improved. He had made friends with the collector and dealer, Paul Durand-Ruel, and was becoming better known.

Monet helped to organise the first Impressionist Exhibition in 1874. In fact it was the bad press about one of Monet's paintings called **Impression – Sunrise**, 1872 (see page 5) which gave its name to the now famous series of exhibitions.

Monet's wife, Camille, gave birth to their second son in 1878 but she became very weak and sadly died in September 1879. After this, Monet threw himself into his work and painted many landscapes and coastal views. He held one-man shows and was beginning to sell well.

In the mid-1870s Monet produced views of the sailing resort of Argenteuil. **Manet** painted him there in the boat he used as a studio on the river (**Monet in his Floating Studio**, 1874, by Edouard Manet). Monet had a confident and rather showy character and Manet has shown him dressed as a well-off middle class painter despite the fact that he was often penniless and depended on the kindness of his friends. His young wife, Camille, sits in the cabin doorway.

Regatta at Argenteuil (1874) by Claude Monet
Musée d'Orsay, Paris, France

Monet loved to produce lots of paintings of the same place. In the late 1870s, the Paris railway station called Saint-Lazare became a firm favourite. In the 1880s and early 1890s Monet painted views of the Normandy coastline. He also painted a series of the Poplar trees on the banks of the River Epte and haystacks at different times of the year. In the 1890s, he painstakingly recorded the effects of light at different times of the day on the Cathedral at Rouen in Northern France. He worked on as many as 12 canvases a day in order to record exactly the changing effects of light and atmosphere.

In 1883, Monet moved to a house at Giverny, 50 miles out of Paris, and lived there with Alice Hoschede and her family. They finally married in 1891 when Alice's first husband died. Monet lived there for the rest of his life and created a garden paradise which became the subject of more than 500 paintings. He created a lily pond with its own Japanese-style bridge. Like many of the Impressionist painters Monet had admired Japanese art all his life and now he had his very own Japanese garden in which he could paint whenever he wanted.

In 1912, Monet developed cataracts on his eyes which made his eyesight weak. He did not have an operation until 1923, but still went on painting. Between 1916 and 1926 Monet worked on a series of large wall paintings called **Waterlilies** (Nympheas) which were commissioned by the French Prime Minister, Georges Clemenceau. The water of the pond is painted as one continuous study in colour with no horizon or shoreline. They remain a lasting monument to Monet's achievement and to the art movement of Impressionism. Although painted from observation, these paintings are the most abstract of his work. They have become an inspiration to future generations of abstract artists. Today the 12 huge panels are hung in the Orangerie Museum in Paris. Monet died in December, 1926, at the age of 86.

The Waterlilies (1915) by Claude Monet

Musée de l'Orangerie, Paris, France

Bathing at La Grenouillère, 1869, by Claude Monet

National Gallery, London, UK

Ideas
- Are there any popular day trip places near you? Riverside or seaside resorts would be ideal spots for you to make your own painted sketches. Try using Monet's technique of sketching in the main parts of your picture with quick dashes of bright paint.

- Make your own painted studies of sunlight on water and reflections of trees, boats and bridges. Experiment with using contrasting complementary colours such as red/green, blue/orange and yellow/purple.

Background

One of the Impressionists' favourite subjects was to show people at leisure. It only took an hour by train to reach the popular riverside resort of La Grenouillère and many people went there at weekends. Monet and Renoir often painted together and, in the late summer of 1869, Monet spent two months there. **Bathing at La Grenouillère** shows a relaxed scene of people bathing and having a good time. Monet is beginning to develop his own particular style and show his fascination for light effects on rippling water.

Between 1871 and 1878, Monet lived with his wife and 2 children in Argenteuil on the River Seine, only 15 minutes by train from Paris. Renoir, Sisley and Manet joined him there and it was one of the most settled and productive times of his life. He had a floating studio (see page 42) from where he made countless paintings at different times of the day on the river.

naturalism, naturalistic – realistic method that attempts to portray nature truthfully.

Content

This is Monet's view of the bathing and boating resort. It had become very popular with weekend trippers from Paris since the 1850s. The resort was on a small island called the 'Île de Croissy', and had a floating restaurant.

Monet may have intended this to be a sketch for a larger painting but now it is seen as a bold example of his Impressionist style. He has created an unusual composition by dividing the picture into two halves with the wooden bridge stretching right across the middle of it. The view he has chosen is like a photographic snapshot that may have been taken by one of the holiday-makers.

Monet is painting from under the shady trees and is looking out towards the brightly lit river beyond the bridge. He focuses on the effects of sunlight on the rippling water.

The rowing boats jostle each other in the foreground and the three people standing on the bridge are sketched in with a few brushstrokes of blue-black paint. Monet has captured their poses well and they give a relaxed, happy feeling to the picture. A group of people are bathing and having fun in the sunlit water beyond them.

Form

The wooden bridge cuts across the middle of the painting and the broad shapes of light and dark above and below this line echo each other. The sunlit area on the far side of the bridge contrasts with the shady area by the boats.

Monet has put the paint on in flat slabs of colour which makes the painting look decorative and at the same time create a *naturalistic* view of the river.

The three people standing on the bridge link the foreground to the horizon line in the distance. They also form a screen for the bathers whose heads are suggested by touches of blue-black paint bobbing around in the water.

On the left of the painting, Monet has used a few swift brush strokes to put in some people by the boathouse and at the water's edge.

Process

Monet used a lot of the new colours that were coming on to the market at this time. Most of the greens, yellows and violet colours were newly manufactured.

Monet used pale tones of violet with green and brown for the boats. He also mixed the *complementary colours* of red and green together to create the darker shadows inside and around the boats. This produces a much more colourful effect than mixing in black to make these darker tones.

The dashes of different shades of blue paint create a sense of depth in the reflections and sunlight effects on the water. Monet has created a different texture for the leaves on the trees by *stippling* the canvas with light touches of different tones of green.

The touches of bright red on the boats in the distance and flowers on the left of the painting create a good contrast to the green areas. They create a happy feeling and make the picture much more lively.

Mood

This painting has the happy, relaxed atmosphere of people enjoying themselves by the water. Monet has focused on portraying the natural environment rather than details of individual people.

Monet's rapid brushstrokes create an attractive patterned surface to the painting. His use of lighter tones on the water produces a dazzling effect of sunlight which contrasts with the darker, shady areas under the trees. His colours harmonise with each other to create a pleasing overall unity of this lively leisure scene.

Saint-Lazare Station (La Gare Saint-Lazare), 1877, by Claude Monet

Fogg Art Museum, Harvard University Art Museums, USA, Bequest from the Collection of Maurice Wertheim, Class 1906

Background

By the 1870s, travel by train had become fast and popular. Parisians commuted from the suburbs into the centre of Paris and 13 million passengers a year used the Saint-Lazare station alone. The railway had become a favourite modern theme for both artists and writers – **Manet, Pissarro, Caillebotte** and **Monet**, all painted the railways. The newly built Saint-Lazare station formed the setting for the realist writer; Emile Zola's novel called *La Bête Humaine* (*The Human Animal*).

Both Caillebotte and Monet painted views of the Saint-Lazare station. Caillebotte painted a view of the bridge over the railway tracks showing people strolling across it in the sunshine (**Le Pont de l'Europe** – The Bridge of Europe, 1876). Monet painted the station from inside, with the train standing on the tracks and steam billowing out of its funnel. Early in 1877, he began working on a series of paintings at the station and by April seven versions were ready to show at the third Impressionist Exhibition.

The analysis which follows is based on Monet's painting of the Saint-Lazare Station which you can see in the Musée d'Orsay, Paris. The Musée d'Orsay version makes a striking contrast with the one above because it shows the station on a very sunlit day.

Ideas

- Find Monet's painting of Saint-Lazare station on the Musée d'Orsay website and compare it with this version. Then experiment with using warm and cool colours such as orange and blue to create shade and sunlight in your own work. Buildings are good subjects for this as they have surfaces where you can show light and shadow around windows and doorways.

- Try to capture your own effects of coloured light on moisture. You don't have to go far – a boiling kettle in a sunlit kitchen can create an excellent subject.

- If you are lucky enough to live near some of the old steam railways, treat yourself to a day trip and make a few sketches at the same time. Take some photos while you're there as these can always be useful records when you're working on a painting back at home.

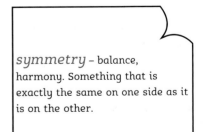

symmetry – balance, harmony. Something that is exactly the same on one side as it is on the other.

Saint-Lazare Station (La Gare Saint-Lazare), 1877, by Claude Monet

Content

When Monet painted the Saint-Lazare station he was living only two minutes away so he could spend most of the day painting there. He was given permission by the Station Master to set up his easel inside the station and trains were even stopped so he had more time to capture a particular effect on his canvas!

This view of the station shows the railway tracks winding towards a train in the centre of the picture. Steam hisses out of it and spreads in puffy clouds under the iron and glass roof. Through the arch of this roof you can see some of the new apartment blocks built by Baron Haussmann in the reconstruction of Paris (see page 12). Dotted around inside the station are railway workers and passengers.

Form

The cast iron and glass roof of the station forms a framework for the picture. It is delicate and strong, a perfect example of new advances in both architecture and technology. The grid of metal supports under the glass roof at the top of the painting carry the eye through to the sunlit modern apartment blocks beyond.

Yellow and orange sunlight pours through the glass roof and mixes with the blue and grey clouds of steam. These freely painted curls of steam and smoke from the train make a good contrast with the rigid *symmetry* of the roof structure. The curving track in the foreground creates a sense of movement in the painting.

Process

Monet built up this railway scene with swift brushstrokes and lots of thick paint. This made the surface of the canvas encrusted and textured with paint. In some places, white and pale colours were dragged across dry layers of textured paint beneath to create steam and smoke effects.

The effects of coloured light on moisture in the atmosphere always fascinated Monet. The cool light inside the station has turned the train's steam a brilliant pale blue which contrasts with the warm colours of the bright sunlight outside.

The painting is built up around the contrast of blue and orange which are complementary opposites in the colour circle. Since the scene is half inside the station and half outside, Monet contrasts warm oranges with cool blue colours to show the effects of sunlight and shadow.

Sunlight also streams through the glass roof and falls on the area in front of the train. The bluish metal tracks and shadows formed by the roof structure create a criss-crossed pattern of blue on orange at the bottom of the painting. Like many of Monet's other paintings this picture is an attractive mixture of patternwork and *naturalism*.

Mood

Monet does not set out to show individual travellers or the hustle and bustle of the crowd at the railway station. He focuses mainly on a strong composition and the varied effects of light.

However, he has created a powerful picture which appeals to our senses. One can almost hear the hiss of the steam from the train and smell the smoke in the air. We can imagine the dazzling sunlight warming us on a spring day, and the colour contrasts and harmonies delight our eye.

His picture remains in our memory as a striking record of the time.

The Waterlily Pond, 1899, by Claude Monet

Private Collection

Ideas

- See how many shades of green you can mix from bluish greens through to yellowy greens.

- Paint a garden scene using as many of these different greens as you can. Be careful to change your brushstrokes to describe the varying textures of plants.

Background

Japanese art and culture had fascinated Monet since he was a young man and he admired prints by Japanese artists such as **Ando Hiroshige**. In 1892, he bought a swampy piece of land near to his house at Giverny and started a project to make his own *oriental* garden. He diverted the River Ru to create a pond and built a Japanese style bridge across it. He planted willow trees, irises and bamboo all along the banks and water lilies covered the surface of the water.

The plants took six years to grow and fully complete Monet's vision. In 1899 he was able to paint the Japanese bridge for the first time and in that year alone he completed 18 views of it. The lily pond itself became the subject of a series of large-scale paintings which are now hung in the Orangerie Gallery in Paris. They were the high point of his career as a painter and a lasting monument to the art of Impressionism.

oriental – coming from the East, e.g. Japan and China.

Content

Most of the views of the Japanese bridge were painted on squarish canvases with the bridge stretching right across the middle of the picture. The strong lines of the bridge contrast with the mass of trees and plants that surround it.

The pond is covered with water lilies and its edges are marked at the side of the painting by reeds and irises. Monet has not painted in a bank to show where the pond ends in the foreground and this gives us a greater feeling of space.

Beyond the bridge trees crowd into the picture and cover the top of the canvas. The bridge helps to create sense of distance in the picture. Without it the painting would lose its feeling of depth and would become a continuous space filled with different shades of green.

Form

In this painting Monet plays around with our sense of space and depth. The bridge is a valuable reference point which enables us to judge where things are in the distance. At the same time, we cannot see its sides or where it joins on to the bank.

The horizontal lines of Monet's bridge cut across the middle of the painting and make us more aware of the painting as a flat patterned surface.

We can work out where the surface of the pond is because of the patches of waterlilies all over it. They form horizontal bands of flowers which go back under the bridge. These bands are cut through by the vertical reflections of the weeping willow trees in the dark areas of water between the lily beds.

Process

Monet uses different kinds of brushwork to create the textures of various plants. Feathery brushstrokes describe the hanging branches of the weeping willow trees and swift dashes of pure colour suggest the pink waterlilies floating on the water's surface.

The whole surface of the pond is like a tapestry. It is painted with a complex network of dashes held together by the vertical lines which represent the reflections of the willow trees.

Monet uses a wide range of greens and yellows. These colours are made more vivid by the touches of pink, red and white in the flowers and the cool blues and violets in the shadows.

Mood

This painting is bursting with the joy of nature's beauty. Monet makes us feel we are standing in the garden ourselves because he brings us so close to so much life and growing plants.

Monet appeals to our senses and we can experience the warm sunshine of a summer's day and hear the birdsong and buzz of insects in this peaceful spot. And yet, Monet remains the observer and we too find ourselves in a thoughtful mood. It seems the more the painting becomes a mirror to Nature, the more we become aware of the painted surface that Monet has constructed for us to gaze at.

Glossary

academic – according to the rules of the academy or university.

alienation – a feeling of being alone and estranged.

anatomy – structure of a body including muscles, skeleton, etc.

anonymous – nameless and unknown.

artificial – not natural.

caricatures – portraits in which features are exaggerated and distorted.

classical – following the rules of art first established in ancient Greece and Rome.

complex – complicated, intricate.

composition – arrangement of the parts of a picture.

complementary colours – colours opposite each other in the colour wheel which create a vibrant effect when placed near to one another. These 'complementary' colours include red/green, yellow/purple and blue/orange.

conservative – a way of thinking that is traditional and unwilling to change.

conventions – rules, set ways of doing things.

creole – descendant of settlers in West Indies.

cropped – cut off at the edge of the frame.

draughtsman – someone who is able to draw well.

dynamic – full of movement, spirited and powerful.

flâneur – a person who strolls about observing people.

fleeting – passing quickly, transient.

foreground – the front area of the picture.

foreshortened – a view of an object which appears to be shorter than it is due to the viewpoint from which it is being drawn.

fragile – delicate, flimsy, dainty.

harmony, harmonies, harmonious – being in agreement, peaceful, not contrasting or jarring.

horizon – line at which the earth and sky appear to meet.

idealised – something which is idealised is shown as the perfect model rather than how it really is.

immediacy – giving the effect of being instant and spontaneous.

impression – vague effect or idea of something.

indifferent – not engaged emotionally.

individual – distinct, unique, special to oneself.

influenced – affected, persuaded, guided by.

intimacy – closeness in personal relationships.

isolated – separate, on one's own.

laundress – a woman who washes and iron clothes.

left wing – a way of thinking that supports the working classes and seeks to bring about a more equal sharing of resources through popular government.

luminous – glowing with light.

manifesto – document which sets out the main aims of a group of artists.

myths – stories often coming from ancient civilisations like Greece and Rome which tell about supernatural beings and happenings.

naturalism, naturalistic – realistic method that attempts to portray nature truthfully.

oriental – coming from the East, e.g. Japan and China.

perspective – a way of constructing a picture from a particular viewpoint as though you were looking through a window into it.

porcelain – delicate kind of clay from which statues or fine china can be made.

realistic – true to life.

shimmering – shining with moving light, glistening, glowing.

snapshot – natural looking photograph taken quickly.

socialist – someone who believes that the community should organise the production of wealth and how it should be spent.

stippling – a painting technique in which the paint is dabbed dryly onto the canvas.

subtle – delicate, mysterious, ingenious.

symmetry – balance, harmony. Something that is exactly the same on one side as it is on the other.

tradition, traditional – ways of doing things which are handed down from one generation to another.

transience – not of a lasting nature.

unorthodox – unconventional, irregular.

vibrant – vivid, thrilling.

wet-in-wet – a painting technique in which the artist does not allow the first layer of paint to dry before adding more paint, usually in a different colour on top.

Timeline

1819 The Realist painter Gustave Courbet is born

1830 Camille Pissarro born

1832 Edouard Manet born

1834 Edgar Degas born

1839 Alfred Sisley and Paul Cézanne born

1840 Claude Monet born

1841 Berthe Morisot, Pierre-Auguste Renoir and Frederic Bazille born

1844 Mary Cassatt born in Pittsburgh, USA

1848 Revolution in France

1848 Gustave Caillebotte born

1862 Monet, Renoir, Sisley and Bazille are students in Charles Gleyre's studio and become great friends

1863 The Salon rejects Manet's painting called **Le Dejeuner sur L'Herbe** and an alternative exhibition is set up called *Salon des Refusés*

1863 Monet, Renoir, Sisley and Bazille make open-air painting trips to the Forest of Fontainbleau and meet the landscape painters of the Barbizon group such as Corot and Pissarro

1865 Manet's painting called **Olympia** is a scandal at the Salon

1870 The Franco-Prussian War begins

1870 Bazille killed in action in the Franco-Prussian War

1871 Franco-Prussian War ends

1871 Pissarro returns from London after the War to find almost all his works have been destroyed by Prussian soldiers

1874 First Impressionist Exhibition

1876 Second Impressionist Exhibition

1877 Third Impressionist Exhibition

1877 Gustave Courbet dies

1879 Fourth Impressionist Exhibition

1879 Renoir's portrait of Madame Charpentier and her children is a huge success at the Salon

1880 Fifth Impressionist Exhibition

1881 Sixth Impressionist Exhibition

1882 Seventh Impressionist Exhibition

1883 Edouard Manet dies

1886 Eighth Impressionist Exhibition

1894 Caillebotte dies

1895 Morisot dies

1899 Sisley dies

1903 Pissarro dies

1906 Cézanne dies

1914 World War 1 begins

1917 Degas dies

1918 World War 1 ends

1919 Renoir dies

1926 Mary Cassatt dies

1926 Claude Monet dies

Resource List

Books for further reading

Impressionism – Art, Leisure, and Parisian Society by Robert L. Herbert, Yale University Press, 1989.

Impressionist Painters by Guy Jennings, Hamlyn, 1986.

Images of Impressionism by Diana Craig, Hamlyn, 1999.

Techniques of the Impressionists by Anthea Callen, New Burlington Books, 1987.

The Painting of Modern Life – Paris in the Art of Manet and his followers by T. J. Clark, Thames and Hudson, 1984.

Impressionist Women by Edward Lucie-Smith, George Weidenfeld and Nicolson Ltd., London, 1989.

The Impressionists by William Gaunt, Thames and Hudson, 1985.

Mary Cassatt by Griselda Pollock, Thames and Hudson, 1998.

Cézanne – Life and Work by Nicola Nonhoff, Konemann, 1999.

Degas by Bernd Growe, Taschen, 2001.

Degas by Keith Roberts, Phaidon Press, 1992.

Manet by John Richardson, Phaidon Press, 1992.

Essential Monet by Vanessa Potts, Parragon, 2000.

Monet by John House, Phaidon, 1992.

Monet's Cathedral – Rouen 1892-1894 by Joachim Pissarro, Pavilion, 1990.

Berthe Morisot by Kathleen Adler and Tamar Garb, Phaidon, 1987.

Renoir – Life and Works by Paul Joannides, Cassell and Co., 2000.

Renoir: His Art, Life and Letters by Barbara White, Harry Abrams, New York, 1988.

Sisley by Richard Shone, Phaidon, 1994.

Useful web sites

www.artchive.com

www.tate.org.uk/modern/default/htm

www.artnet.com

Photographic Credits

Images on these pages appear by kind permission of the following: